65808462R00111

Made in the USA
Columbia, SC
14 July 2019